Business Plan Write-Up and Pitch
General Construction Machine Tools
Business Start-Up

Table of Contents

1. Executive Summary

a. Service/Product Summary

The industry is construction but the market is machine tooling. The market in Toronto, Ontario is relatively stable, although its size, workmanship and revenue may fluctuate from time to time. The objective of this particular business plan is turn demonstrate the turnaround of initial investment, projected at three years or less. The business owner plans to open this enterprise with advanced machining techniques, unique tools and innovations, and unparalleled customer service, which will get him into the market and well into competitive status. The company will offer a specific set of services in the Canadian machining industry, which will evolve and diversify in three stages as the business matures.

b. Uniquely Qualified

i. Unique Management Team

This company is led by Michael Shiojda, a market leader with over 25 years of experience in the machining industry. With previous business experience as a welding and machine shop operator at Custom Components, Mr. Shiojda is well-qualified to lead the operations of this new machining startup. Mr. Shiojda's particular industry specialties include:

- Assembling and operating machine tools including lathes, mills, grinders, hexes and broaching
- Thermoforming and injection plastic mold design

- Machine parts manufacturing using oxygen-propane and plasma torch-cutting techniques
- Mechanical systems assembly and maintenance
- Industrial equipment assembly and repair

Mr. Shiojda's educational qualifications in this industry include diplomas from ICS Canada and Centennial College in electrical and mechanical engineering. His formal education at these institutions covered tool design, CNC operation and programming, auto CAD and Inventor-3D design, as well as fluid and compressed air mechanics.

He is knowledgeable about health and safety in the workplace, having completed WHMIS and H2S training. In addition to his educational and work safety qualifications, Mr. Shiojda's leading roles at KG Machine Co., Industrial Equipment Design Co., Custom Components and Mold & Tools Inc. leave him with insider knowledge and a competitive edge in the industry. Not only does he have knowledge and experience in overhauling and renewing spare parts, he is skilled in customizing machine parts in order to deliver specialized, custom machining services that set his business apart from others in the industry.

ii. First in the Industry

Our company is the first in the industry to combine existing machine overhauling, custom parts manufacturing and metal equipment production all in one shop. Our diversified services along with our niche specialty of custom metal stair railing manufacturing, installation and maintenance insure that we are unique in the industry.

Mr. Shiojda's experience of working with local production companies and builders gives him a wide professional network from which to draw professional clients. His insider knowledge of the building requirements and operations of these businesses leave him uniquely qualified to provide them with his machining services. The personal relationships Mr. Shiojda has built up with professional builders over the years will allow him and his company to corner a specific corner of the market, with a particular focus on manufacturing and maintaining metal stair railings.

c. Synopsis of Financial Projection

i. *Expected Revenue*

Businesses in the Canadian machining industry are generally profitable, with 77.9% of them having turned a profit in the 2012 census year[1]. The overall industry averages are profitable, with average total revenue at $709,300/year, and average total expenses at $643,900/year. For profitable firms, net profits averaged $98,100 for micro and small machine shop businesses.

ii. *Expenses and Profits – 5 Years*

The cost of sales (direct expenses) for this operation includes the cost of wages, benefits, purchases of materials and supplies, and inventory costs. The industry average cost of sales in 2011 was $392,500, which accounted for 55.3% of total revenues [2].

The operating expenses (indirect costs) of this operation include loan amortization, utilities, rent, interest and bank charges, advertising and promotional costs, insurance, delivery and warehouse expenses and other expenses. Industry average costs for operating expenses were $251,500 in 2011, which accounted for 35.5% of total revenue.

This company needs only six main machines to begin operations, and will employ only the minimum number of employees to get started, which will categorize it as a micro

---

[1] Statistics Canada, special tabulation, unpublished data, Small Business Profiles. Accessed from:
https://www.ic.gc.ca/app/scr/sbms/sbb/cis/benchmarking.html?code=33271&lang=eng
[2] According to NAICS industry code 33271

4

business. In phase one of operations, the company will hire one permanent employee and up to three temporary employees to account for seasonal fluctuations and changes in supply and demand. This will help keep costs low to begin with as the company establishes its share of the market.

Expenses Year 1

Cost of Sales	Total ($)
Wages	60,000
Machine startup costs	150,000
Materials	20,000
Inventory	5,000
Total Cost of Sales	**235,000**
Operating Expenses	Total
Rent	25,000
Utilities	10,000
Advertising and promotions	2,000
Insurance	4,000
Total Operating Expenses	**41,000**

Total Expenses (Year One)	276,000

Total expenses for year one total $276,000, which is well below the industry average of $656,900. The majority of these costs will go towards the acquisition of the six basic machines necessary for the operation of this business (outlined in part iv. *Use of Funds*), which is a one-time startup cost of $150,000.

Year 3

Total expenses for year 3 will include maintenance and amortization costs of $10,000 for the six machines, and will exclude their startup cost. To allow for increased business operations, wages expenditure will increase to 100,000, and materials expenditure to 40,000. Allowing for increases in rent and utilities costs, total expenses for year 3 are estimated at around $200,000.

Year 5

Company expenses will be adjusted to accommodate market demand. If the company continues to expand and attract new customers and projects, potential expenses for year 5 are budgeted at up to $300,000.

Net Profit

Year One: Due to the minimum $150,000 investment in startup machinery, the company expects only to break even in year one.

Year Three: Startup investment starts to see a return, and increased customers bring in more revenue.

Year Five: The company continues to expand and increase its market share, attracting new customers and contracts and approaches industry average revenues.

iii. Seeking Funding of

This company is seeking $250,000 to begin startup business operations and initiate phase one of company growth.

iv. Use of Funds

In order to get this company off the ground, we need a minimum of six large-scale machines to begin operations. These six machines will ensure that we can offer a wide range of services which will appeal to the largest customer base possible, and also allow us to offer specific machining services that are unique to the industry. Offering a variety of both broadly focused and unique custom services will ensure our successful entry into the Ontario machining market we are targeting for the first phase of our company's operations. The six machines that we need to start the first phase of our operations are:

1) One medium size lathe machine (minimum 6 feet)

2) *One medium size milling machine, preferably one produced by the Bridgeport milling brand*

3) *One medium size surface grinder for table work (minimum size 24 by 12 to 30 by 16 inches)*

4) *One regular standing drill press*

5) *One medium size MIG or Stick welding machine*

6) *One medium size TIG welding machine*

At an average cost of $25,000 for each of the six machines we need to get started, the machine startup costs for this company total $150,000.

In addition to the machinery costs, the startup funds being requested will be used to cover the costs associated with starting up phase one of company operations.

2. Company Overview

a. When and how will the organization be formed

We believe in growing this company sustainably, from the ground up. In order to develop the business in a way that progresses slowly and steadily, three stages of company operation have been planned. Moving forward through these three stages will ensure that the business expands in a way that is successful, stable and profitable.

- *Stage One*: The company will enter the Canadian machining market and establish itself as a key player by offering services that are customized and unique to the industry
  - In this stage, the machining shop will serve production companies with regular maintenance services to keep their machines and equipment finely-tuned and operating at peak performance
  - As we establish relationships with regular large-scale customers, we will give suggestions for ways equipment and machinery can be improved and refined, offering customers the option to replace standard parts with our own customized parts
  - In addition to creating our own parts, the shop will use six key pieces of equipment (outlined below) to service the machinery of our clients
- *Stage Two:* In stage two, the company continues to provide maintenance services while stepping up the production side of the business
  - 25 years of experience in this industry has led the company director to

10

realize that one of the main problems in the machining industry is a lack of suitable equipment to tackle tricky jobs that service highly specialized equipment

- In order to meet this market demand, the company will act on ideas for new equipment parts whenever a suitable piece of equipment is difficult to find
- When new equipment prototypes are seen to be successful n 90% or more of cases, and a high market demand is determined to exist, the shop will continue production of this customized part
- This new production side of the company will be supported by phase one once the shop has enough regular clients to become financially solvent

o *Stage Three:* Transition into a production company

- With the continuing financial support of regular, long-term clients requiring basic machine maintenance needs in stage one, and if prototypes of stage two are successful, the company will transition into a production company
- Prototypes that prove to be 90% effective or more will be manufactured by our company, leading to the creation of our own in-house line of customized machinery products, completely unique to the industry

- Incorporate the business

- Create a logo

- Secure an ideal location for the main shop

- Develop and distribute marketing materials and contact network of clients

- Obtain six essential startup machines

- Begin Phase One

- Assess profitability and move on to Phase Two

- Assess profitability and move on to Phase Three

3. Industry Analysis

a. Market Overview

The machining industry in Canada currently consists predominantly of independent businesses, with no single company or corporation having achieved a dominant market share or monopoly. The national machine shop industry is focused largely in Ontario, which holds 44.8% of the market share[3]. The industry is characterized by micro businesses (1-4 employees), which comprise 39.9% of the market, and small businesses (5-99 employees), which make up 58.9% of the market. For most of its operations, this company will be a micro business, with 1 to 3 employees working under the guidance of Mr. Shiojda.

Companies within the Canadian machining industry draw in revenue by operating, manufacturing and repairing machine tools, metal parts and machine equipment. These tools may include any or all of the following:

- Manual and computer-operated lathes
- Computer numerical control (CNC) milling machines
- automatic screw machines
- bores and drilling machines
- grinders

---

[3] Statistics Canada, Canadian Business Patterns Database, December 2012. Accessed from: https://www.ic.gc.ca/app/scr/sbms/sbb/cis/establishments.html?code=33271&lang=eng

- general and custom metal-working machines

Some companies operate these machine tools for individual clients as part of their own business operations, while others primarily manufacture and/or repair machining tools and custom metal parts to be sold up the market to larger machining companies. The products and services offered by this industry include:

- Drilling and boring services
- Sawing
- EDM and ECM activities
- Turning services to produce cylindrical components
- Grinding and planning services
- Fastening services using automatic screw machines

Thanks to these important services, small to medium sized companies in the Canadian machining industry play a pivotal role in some of this nation's larger industries, such as auto manufacturing, drilling and construction, forestry, mining, and natural resource extraction.

b. Relevant Market Size

In the 2012 census year, there were 3,818 machine shops operating in Canada, with 1,128 of them (44.8%) operating in Ontario[4]. The revenue bracket of the Canadian

---

[4] Statistics Canada, Canadian Business Patterns Database, December 2012. Accessed from https://www.ic.gc.ca/app/scr/sbms/sbb/cis/establishments.html?code=33271&lang=eng

machining industry is $6 billion dollars per annum, and the growth rate of this market is currently pegged at 3.9% per year. There are 4,226 businesses currently operating in this industry, and they employ over 35,000 permanent employees nation-wide.

4. Customer Analysis

a. Target Customers

Primary customers: large-scale production companies and companies previously worked for by Mr. Shiojda, who has specialized knowledge of their strengths, weaknesses and needs. Particular focus on manufacturing and maintaining metal stair railings customized to the specifications of company builders.

Secondary customers: walk-ins and individual clients

b. Customer Needs

Customers of Mr. Shiojda's business need a machinist with specialized knowledge of their processes, and the tools and know-how necessary to manufacture and maintain their metal stair railings and other parts.

5. Competitive Analysis

a. Direct Competitors

Since there are no major monopolies or corporations involved in this specific industry, our main competitors are other independent small machining businesses. Those located close by will be of most competition, but our prices and unique services will out-compete them.

b. Indirect Competitors

Indirect competitors for some of our parts manufacturing include large retailers like Canadian Tire and Home Depot, and some machines can receive basic maintenance in mechanics' shops. However, our products, services and manufacturing are much more specialized than what either of these indirect competitors can provide.

c. Competitive Advantages

Allies: The business's existing contacts will be utilized to create word-of-mouth communication about our services and direct customers and clients to our specialized services. We will stand out from the crowd with our many years of experience and ability to create customized machine parts to meet the standards of any job. By offering specialized as well as diversified services, we can capture an optimal corner of the market.

Niche services: We are experts in metal stair railings, and can manufacture and repair them better than anyone in the industry. In addition, our overhaul old machines and create new, customized parts makes us stand out from the crowd

Diversified services and customer base: By offering a wide range of services from general to specific makes us perfect for any job that comes our way. At the same time, servicing a diversity of clients who are differentiated by size, industry and geography insulates us against downturns in any one industry and provides us with multiple revenue streams.

17

Unique ideas: Our vision is flexible and creative, important industry qualities, yet also sustainable. We see ourselves innovating new products and eventually launching a custom production line, hopefully within 5 years. However, we always have an eye on the bottom line, and will be accordingly flexible in moving through our anticipated three stages of business growth.

Streamlined business model: Compared to our competitors, we have a more streamlined approach to this business. We prioritize jobs, keep a tight production schedule, and are as isolated as possible from outside suppliers. This gives us a competitive advantage over the market.

6. Marketing Plan

a. Products and Services

Primary service: Using six industry standard machines to manufacture and service custom metal parts

Focus: Custom metal stair railings

Secondary services: machine maintenance and repair, custom parts and metal equipment manufacturing

b. Pricing Model

The company will provide clients with a quoted estimate for services required on a per-project basis. Pricing will be equal to or lower than the industry standard, and prices will be matched if a client finds a lower price elsewhere.

Customers of the company will be able to open an account based on their proper credit, and will receive invoices once they have reached 75% of their credit.

By utilizing Mr. Shiojda's network of personal business contacts, pricing will be negotiated at a fair price in a familiar environment that competing shops can't offer.

To promote our services, the company will utilize location, specialized services and business networking, as well as promotional materials and discounts.

Target market: By specializing in the manufacture and maintenance of metal stair railings, the company will hone in on a specific niche market, and utilize existing industry connections to draw in a large number of clients right from the beginning. Once clients in this niche market are satisfied with our services, the rest of our diversified service package will be available to them.

To advertise our services, memos will be sent out to all existing production company and builder contacts to inform them of our products and services, and invite them for a free consultation. Ads will be placed via social media on Facebook, Twitter, and Google+, as well as in local business listings and the yellow pages. The company car will be painted with the company name, logo, and phone number, to advertise to potential new customers around the clock, and the shop front will be kept neat and welcoming. Cold calls will be made to potential local clients if appropriate, and customer service and satisfaction will be made top priority at all times.

7. Operations Plan

a. Key Operational Processes (Customer Service Department)

In order to operate, the company will require supplies from local suppliers, as follows:

General tools	Canadian Tire, Home Depot
General materials	Home Depot
Specialized tools and materials	Princess Auto, H D Brafasco, Fastenal
Molds, bearings and steel suppliers	Custom

8. Financial Plan

PRO FORMA PROFIT AND LOSS			
	2000	**2001**	**2002**
Sales	$1,960,000	$4,060,000	$5,260,000
Direct Cost of Sales	$400,000	$827,000	$1,069,000
Production Personnel	$350,040	$600,000	$650,000
TOTAL COST OF SALES	**$750,040**	**$1,427,000**	**$1,719,000**
Gross Margin	$1,209,960	$2,633,000	$3,541,000
Gross Margin %	61.73%	64.85%	67.32%
Expenses			
Payroll	$285,000	$310,000	$350,000
Marketing/Promotion	$167,900	$220,000	$265,000
Depreciation	$9,996	$30,000	$40,000
Quality Assurance	$93,800	$104,000	$125,000
General & Administrative	$96,000	$124,000	$174,000
Manufacturing & Engineering	$129,600	$130,000	$175,000
Machining & Systems Building	$86,400	$100,000	$110,000
Payroll Taxes	$0	$0	$0
Other	$0	$0	$0
Total Operating Expenses	$868,696	$1,018,000	$1,239,000
Profit Before Interest and Taxes	$341,264	$1,615,000	$2,302,000
EBITDA	$351,260	$1,645,000	$2,342,000
Interest Expense	$47,705	$29,150	$12,470
Taxes Incurred	$74,621	$396,463	$581,922
Net Profit	$218,938	$1,189,388	$1,707,608
Net Profit/Sales	11.17%	29.30%	32.46%

www.ingramcontent.com/pod-product-compliance
Lightning Source LLC
Chambersburg PA
CBHW051830170526
45167CB00005B/2220